Let's Play Hopscotch

By Anita Khan

Illustrated by
Lindy Burnett

Target Skill Review

Scott Foresman
is an imprint of

PEARSON

Toss it, Ann. Two.

Jump two spots, Ann.

Toss it, Lil. One.

Hop one spot, Lil.

Drop it, Ann. Four.

Next skip to four, Ann.

Drop it, Lil. Five.

Next jump to five, Lil.

Toss it, Ann. Six.

Hop to six, Ann.

Toss it, Lil. Ten.

Skip to ten, Lil.

Look! Ann got to ten.

Come on, Lil. I will help.